The NASTY paSt

By
John Wood

CRiMe

BookLife
PUBLISHING

©2022
BookLife Publishing Ltd.
King's Lynn
Norfolk, PE30 4LS, UK

All rights reserved.
Printed in Poland.

A catalogue record for this book is
available from the British Library.

ISBN: 978-1-80155-548-7

Written by:
John Wood

Edited by:
Emilie Dufresne

Designed by:
Dan Scase

All facts, statistics, web addresses
and URLs in this book were verified
as valid and accurate at time of
writing. No responsibility for any
changes to external websites or
references can be accepted by
either the author or publisher.

PHOTO CREDITS

Front cover – ilolab, kaer_stock, Joy Rector, andersphoto, Labusova Olga, Fer Gregory, Lerner Vadim.
4 – Vladimir Mulder, CRS PHOTO. 5 – Ttatty. 6 – Dirk M. de Boer, proslgn, Fer Gregory. 7 – Otar Gujejiani, LifetimeStock. 8 – guidopiano, Hal_P. 9 –
frankie's, peresanz. 10 – Andrey Burmakin, Steve Bramall. 11 – Gorodenkoff, Dmitrijs Bindemanis. 12 – Arkadiusz Fajer, OSTILL is Franck Camhi. 13
– ratsadapong rittinone, Trofimov Denis. 14 – Alla Berlezova, meunierd, Atomazul. 15 – Everett Collection, meunierd. 16 – Philip Sidney, Songquan
Deng. 17 – Sirocco, Peter R Foster IDMA, Christopher Elwell. 18 – txking, Joseph Smeeton, Auguste Tilly (graveurs). 19 – Stephm2506. 20 – Photo-
Art-Lortie, Wikicommons, FBI. 21 – William R Casey, Everett Historical. 22 – tommaso lizzul, thekovtun. 23 – Soare Cecilia Corina, Cris Foto. 24 –
Stokkete, charles taylor. 25 – Jose_vdhd_Photography, yavyav. 26 – travelview, Martin Mehes. 27 – Dee Browning, victorgrigas. 28 – Sergio Foto,
Studio 36. 29 – Evannovostro, Chubykin Arkady. 30 – Sergio Foto, Studio 36. Header banners – Novikov Alex. Blood prints – Oksana Mizina. Blood
drips – ALEXSTAND. Backgrounds – ilolab, Groundback Atelier, Krasovski Dmitri, Groundback Atelier. Photo borders – Welena, Krasovski Dmitri.
Stone captions – Philll. Wooden Fact Boxes – My Life Graphic. Blood headings – Olha Burlii. Finger Print – Andrey_Kuzmin. Images are courtesy
of Shutterstock.com. With thanks to Getty Images, Thinkstock Photo and iStockphoto.

Contents

Words that look like **THIS** are explained in the glossary on page 31.

A Discovery from the Past

There are secrets underground. It's not all dirt and mud, especially if you know where to look. Buried under all that earth and rock are clues to the past. Whether it's bones, bodies, books or weapons, each clue tells a story of something that happened a long time ago. And it turns out that these stories can be pretty gruesome...

The people who find and study old, historical objects are called archaeologists (say: ar-kee-ol-uh-jists).

The past wasn't a friendly place. People didn't live as long as they do now, and there were plenty of things to kill them before they even reached old age. Towns were dirty, work was brutal, and disease and war were everywhere. Despite all this, people still made pottery and jewellery, built homes and temples, and lived their lives. Some of the things they made are still in the earth with their bones,

It might not seem like it, but

A NEW STORY

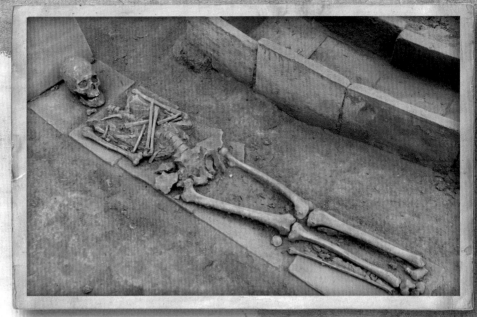

Here in this museum, all sorts of objects are collected so people can learn about history. There are even old skeletons of people who died long ago. Look, here is one! This skeleton is missing its hands. The bones look very old and worn. This person probably lived between A.D. 476 and 1400. The skeleton was found in Europe. Who were they, and how did they die? Did this person **COMMIT** a crime all those years ago?

To find out exactly how this person met their end, you must travel through history. Take a note of each crime you learn about and see if any of them might explain our skeleton here. But be careful – the past can be very, very dangerous.

Ching Shih

Who was the most fearsome pirate that ever lived? Who had the most ships, and **COMMANDED** the most people? Was it Blackbeard? Was it Barbarossa, which means Red Beard in Italian? What if you found out that the most fearsome pirate didn't have a beard at all?

MEET CHING SHIH

Ching Shih, one of the greatest pirates in history, was unknown in the early years of her life. Historians have found very few **RECORDS** of her childhood. However, historians do know that she was born in the Guangdong province of China in 1775. At some point she married a pirate called Zheng Yi. Nobody is sure if Zheng Yi captured her, or if he just asked her to marry him. Either way, in 1801, Zheng Yi and Ching Shih became husband and wife, and together they controlled the Red Flag Fleet. They agreed that they would both have equal power. Under their control, the Red Flag Fleet grew from around 200 ships to 1,700 ships.

The Red Flag Fleet had around 50,000 pirates in it.

Ching Shih became known as 'The Terror of South China'. Many people thought that she couldn't be defeated.

Six years after their marriage, Zheng Yi died. Ching Shih became leader herself, with Zheng Yi's second-in-command Chang Pao to assist her. The Red Flag Fleet sailed the oceans, robbing towns and other ships. Ching Shih created lots of rules for her pirates; any treasure that they found would be split among the whole fleet (although the ship that found it would get more than the rest). Any prisoners who were women were let go, unless a pirate wanted to marry her. However, Ching Shih made sure that no women were hurt, and that no pirate married more than one woman. If a pirate broke these rules, they would be whipped, killed or have something chopped off.

Pirates who ran away from the Red Flag Fleet would get their ears cut off!

A TRUCE

The Chinese **GOVERNMENT** wasn't powerful enough to stop the pirates. Eventually, a deal was made: the pirates would respect the government and stop their life of crime on the seas, and in return they would get to keep all their treasure. Ching Shih agreed, and she lived the rest of her life in peace.

The Chinese, Portuguese and British governments all tried to take Ching Shih and her pirates down. However, none of them could do it.

Jack the Ripper

In 1888, the people of London, England, were scared. There was a killer on the loose. He was known as Jack the Ripper, and he would wander the streets at night, looking for victims. Between August and November, it is thought that Jack the Ripper killed five or six people. However, he was never caught, and it remains a mystery that people are still trying to solve today.

A GRISLY WAY TO GO

Police thought that Jack the Ripper had a job, because he only murdered at the weekend. They thought he might be 'frighteningly normal' on the outside.

There were five murders that the police were certain were done by Jack the Ripper. There was also a sixth murder that may have been committed by the Ripper, but nobody knows for sure. All of them were women, and most of them older women. Jack the Ripper committed these crimes in the dead of night, when few people were around. He usually chopped up his victims using a long, sharp knife. The London police thought that he must have been a doctor or a butcher because he was so skilled with a knife.

LONDON

PANIC ON THE STREETS OF LONDON

Newspapers around the world ran stories on Jack the Ripper, reporting the killings. This made many people even more frightened. The police received dozens of letters that were signed by 'Jack the Ripper'. In these letters, the killer promised to strike again, and said that the police would never catch him. However, many historians think that these were not written by the real killer, but from people playing tricks. The panic became so widespread that **MOBS** would chase criminals through the streets if they thought it was Jack the Ripper.

Jack the Ripper was thought to be medium height, with a **STOCKY** build.

The **INVESTIGATION** of Jack the Ripper began a new way of doing police work. For example, police took a photo at the crime scene of his fifth victim, Mary Jane Kelly. Nowadays, pictures are taken at every crime scene to help solve the case. Today, police are much better at finding and stopping criminals. Jack the Ripper would never stand a chance now.

This is Whitechapel. Most of the murders took place here or nearby.

Robin Hood

According to the stories, Robin Hood was an **OUTLAW** who lived in England around the 12th century. Robin Hood was a skilled fighter, especially with a bow and arrow. He lived in Sherwood Forest alongside other outlaws called his Merry Men, and they wore bright green clothes. As silly as they might have looked, the outlaws were feared. They were famous for stealing money from the rich and giving it to the poor.

The stories of Robin Hood are legends – this means they are stories that may have been partly true at one time.

Even though stealing is a crime, Robin Hood is seen as a hero. This is because, in the stories, England was an unfair place. The evil Sheriff of Nottingham created unfair laws and made people pay high taxes. This left most people much poorer. However, Robin Hood attacked and robbed rich people, and shared out all the gold he took. This meant that **PEASANTS** could afford to buy things such as clothes and food. There are lots of tales of Robin Hood's adventures, from battling soldiers in the forest to tricking the King. However, did any of it really happen? Did Robin Hood ever exist?

According to the stories, when Robin Hood was dying, he shot a final arrow from his bow. He asked to be buried wherever the arrow landed.

SHERWOOD FOREST

THE REAL ROBIN

Historians do not have any solid **EVIDENCE** to prove when Robin Hood lived and what he did. Records show that criminals and outlaws often called themselves Robin Hood, or similar names such as 'Robehod' or 'Rabunhod'. This may have been because of his legend, or because they knew of a real Robin Hood. However, even if he was real, the truth would have been very different to the stories. For example, in the early tales, there isn't any talk of robbing the rich and giving to the poor at all!

Robin Hood and his Merry Men were probably much more **VIOLENT** than they were portrayed in later stories. In one early record, one of the merry men kills someone to stop their band being discovered. That doesn't sound like something a hero would do!

Some historians think that an outlaw called Robert of Wetherby was the first Robin Hood. Little is known about Robert of Wetherby, but he was very famous at the time. Other historians think that a man called Hereward the Wake might have been an inspiration. Like Robin Hood, Hereward was an outlaw who was very good at **DISGUISES**. However, Hereward was much more blood-thirsty – he is said to have killed 14 men with the help of only one follower.

As usual, the past is much gorier in real life than it is told in the stories...

11

Edmond Locard

Edmond Locard was known as the Sherlock Holmes of France. He changed the way police investigated crime scenes. Locard was very interested in solving crimes scientifically, which meant relying on clues, instead of only listening to **WITNESSES**. He believed that police could find evidence of a crime and use that to prove what happened and, more importantly, who did it.

Locard had read lots of Sherlock Holmes books. When he was a teacher, he told his students to read the stories too.

Locard was born in 1877 in Lyon, France. He was very clever; by 1907 he had learnt how to become both a doctor and a lawyer. In 1908, he decided to travel the world, visiting police departments in Germany, Italy, Switzerland and the United States of America. In World War One, Locard worked with the French Secret Service. He was able to tell how soldiers had died by studying their uniforms for clues. In his life, he wrote many books which are still talked about today.

Locard also researched fingerprints. Everybody has their own special fingerprint. This means that if police find fingerprints at a crime scene, it can tell them who has been there.

Locard's most important idea was his 'exchange principle'. This sounds complicated, but all it means is that something is passed between two things that touch. Locard said this meant that criminals leave a trace of themselves at the crime scene, and a crime scene leaves a trace on the criminal. Traces of a criminal can include all sorts of things, such as fingerprints, hair, blood and pieces of clothing. These traces could lead the police to the criminal.

Poor Locard spent his whole life looking for the blood, hair and grubby fingerprints of criminals. Gross.

Locard used his exchange principle in 1912. A woman named Marie Latelle was found dead. Her boyfriend, Emile Gourbin, said he had been playing cards with his friends at the time, so it couldn't have been him. Locard examined Marie's body and saw that she had been strangled. Then, he scraped underneath Emile's fingernails and found traces of women's makeup. Locard found a **CHEMIST** who told him that it matched Marie's makeup, and Emile soon **CONFESSED** to the murder.

Emile had tricked his friends by changing the time on the clock, so they thought they were playing cards at the same time as the murder. However, he couldn't trick Locard.

The Wild West

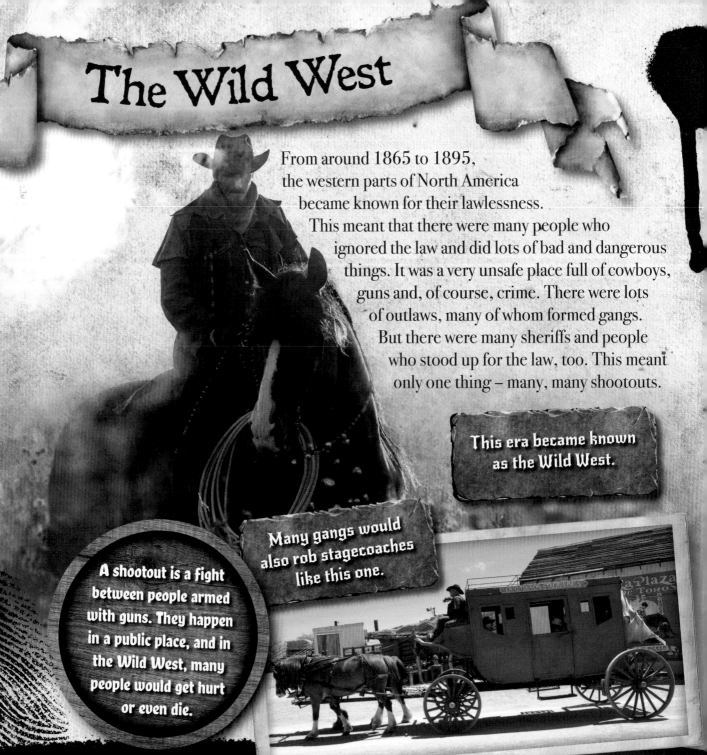

From around 1865 to 1895, the western parts of North America became known for their lawlessness. This meant that there were many people who ignored the law and did lots of bad and dangerous things. It was a very unsafe place full of cowboys, guns and, of course, crime. There were lots of outlaws, many of whom formed gangs. But there were many sheriffs and people who stood up for the law, too. This meant only one thing – many, many shootouts.

This era became known as the Wild West.

Many gangs would also rob stagecoaches like this one.

A shootout is a fight between people armed with guns. They happen in a public place, and in the Wild West, many people would get hurt or even die.

THE GUNFIGHT AT O.K. CORRAL

The most famous shootout in all of the Wild West happened in a town called Tombstone. In 1881, a **FEUD** had grown between a bunch of outlaws called the Clanton gang and the three Earp brothers: Wyatt, Morgan and Virgil. The shootout happened at a building called the O.K. Corral. Although it only lasted around 30 seconds, three outlaws were killed, and the Earp brothers became famous.

THE WILD BUNCH

The Wild Bunch was a collection of over 200 outlaws. They were led by one of the most famous outlaws of all time, a man named Butch Cassidy. They made most of their money by robbing trains and banks. They had three hideouts around the states of Wyoming and New Mexico, called The Hole in the Wall, Brown's Hole and Robber's Roost. Each of these were hidden in valleys and canyons that were hard to get to.

MISSOURI CENTRAL

14

There must be an easier way to make money than this.

BILLY THE KID

One of the most feared gunmen in the Wild West was Billy the Kid. As a child, he moved to Kansas with his parents, but then started to spend time with outlaws. He roamed the southern part of the US and northern Mexico as a thief and an outlaw. In 1880, he was captured and **SENTENCED** to be **HANGED**. However, he escaped and went on the run. Eventually he was tracked down and shot. Billy the Kid was only 21 years old at the time.

It is said that Billy the Kid killed at least 27 people in his life.

WANTED
DEAD or ALIVE

BILLY THE KID
WILLIAM BONNEY
$5,000 REWARD

NOTIFY- Marshall Pat Garrett

15

Guy Fawkes

One of the most famous criminals in Britain didn't even get a chance to commit his crime. His name was Guy Fawkes. He was part of a group who planned to blow up the English Houses of Parliament, on the 5th of November, 1605. Many important people would have been in the building at the time, including many members of Parliament (MPs), the royal family and the King. The plan became known as the Gunpowder Plot.

NOT A BANG, BUT A WHIMPER

At the time, England was ruled by Protestants; these were people who followed a type of RELIGION called Protestantism. Guy Fawkes and his crew were Catholics, who followed a religion called Catholicism.

Guy Fawkes and his group had it all figured out. They stashed 36 barrels of gunpowder and piles of firewood in the basement of the Houses of Parliament. Guy Fawkes was in charge of setting the gunpowder on fire, which would cause it to explode, killing everyone inside and destroying the entire building. However, as he waited outside the basement, matches in his pocket, he was discovered! Someone had sent a letter warning the government and royal family about the plan. Guy Fawkes was arrested and the gunpowder was taken away.

Houses of Parliament

WHO WAS GUY FAWKES?

Guy Fawkes was born in the north of England, in 1570. He was a Catholic, and he moved to Spain in around 1593 to become a soldier. When he returned, he was invited to join a group of men who were going to carry out the Gunpowder Plot. The group was led by a man called Robert Catesby. Guy Fawkes was just the guy with the matches.

This is what gunpowder is meant to do, Mr Fawkes! You had one job!

When he was caught, Guy Fawkes said his name was John Johnson, and refused to speak further. However, after being tortured for days, he told the truth about the plan and all the other people who were involved. There is no record of exactly what kind of torture was used, but afterwards Guy Fawkes was only just alive. Then, on the 31st of January, 1606, Guy Fawkes was hanged, drawn and quartered. This meant he was dangled with a rope around his neck, had his insides cut out, and was then chopped into four pieces.

In England, Guy Fawkes is remembered every year on the 5th of November. To celebrate stopping the massive explosion, everyone sets off massive explosions of their own - fireworks!

People also burn figures of Guy Fawkes on giant bonfires.

A Reason for Crime

Throughout most of history, the answer to crime was pretty simple. If somebody broke the law, they would be **PUNISHED** in a horrible way. However, in the 19th century, some people began to wonder if there was a link between crimes and the kind of people that committed them. Were some people more likely to be criminals? Why?

Choosing a life of crime could see you doing jail time...

ADOLPHE QUETELET

Adolphe Quetelet was born in Belgium, in February 1796. He was very good at maths, and he used this skill to collect information on crimes in Belgium and the Netherlands. He looked at the types of crimes being committed and who was committing them. He recorded all sorts of things, such as their age, how rich or poor they were and if they were male or female. His work showed that many criminals came from poorer areas, and they didn't have much money growing up. Life was usually harder and more unfair for them, so they turned to a life of crime.

ADOLPHE QUETELET

CESARE LOMBROSO

Cesare Lombroso, who was born in 1835, was an Italian criminologist (say: crim-in-ol-uh-jist) – this meant that he studied crime. Lombroso thought that there was a certain type of person who broke the law, and that these people were more **PRIMITIVE**. To prove that these people were different, Lombroso examined over 400 dead criminals. He found that there were certain **TRAITS** that were found in a lot of criminals. For example, he said that criminals had bigger ears, messier teeth, differently-shaped skulls and wonky faces.

There's nothing wrong with having big ears, Lombroso.

CESARE LOMBROSO

Unfortunately, Lombroso was wrong about a lot of things. Nobody is born a criminal. Since his work, many people have pointed out that criminals might have those traits because of their lifestyle. For example, if you got in fights all the time, you might have a wonky, broken nose. However, that doesn't mean all people with wonky noses are going to be criminals. However, even though Lombroso was wrong about a lot of stuff, he was right to look for reasons to explain why people break the law. Knowing why people commit crimes can help police stop them in the first place.

Bonnie and Clyde

Bonnie Parker met Clyde Barrow in Texas, 1930, when she was 19 years old and he was 21. They fell in love. However, Clyde was arrested for burglary soon after and sent to prison. Bonnie visited him every day until he escaped using a gun which she **SMUGGLED** into the prison for him. After Clyde went in and out of prison again, the couple finally ran away together to live a life of crime in 1934.

Apparently, going to the cinema wasn't exciting enough for this couple.

ON THE RUN

Over the next two years, the couple joined many gangs to carry out robberies at banks and stores. The police saw them as ruthless – they would kill anyone who got in their way. However, most people seemed to like them, and saw them as heroic criminals like Robin Hood. A huge search began; wanted posters with Bonnie and Clyde's pictures were put up all over the place. The newspapers were full of stories about the pair.

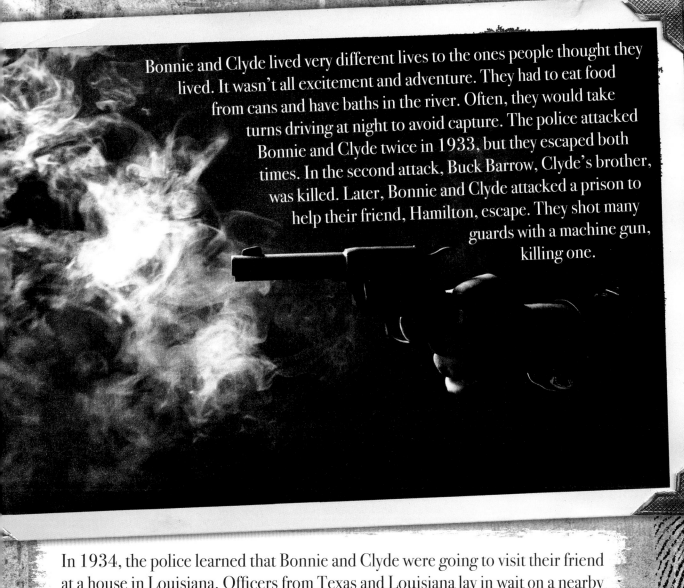

Bonnie and Clyde lived very different lives to the ones people thought they lived. It wasn't all excitement and adventure. They had to eat food from cans and have baths in the river. Often, they would take turns driving at night to avoid capture. The police attacked Bonnie and Clyde twice in 1933, but they escaped both times. In the second attack, Buck Barrow, Clyde's brother, was killed. Later, Bonnie and Clyde attacked a prison to help their friend, Hamilton, escape. They shot many guards with a machine gun, killing one.

In 1934, the police learned that Bonnie and Clyde were going to visit their friend at a house in Louisiana. Officers from Texas and Louisiana lay in wait on a nearby road, waiting for the chance to ambush the pair. When Bonnie and Clyde showed up, the police opened fire! The criminals' car was covered in bullet holes and Bonnie and Clyde were killed.

Bonnie and Clyde's Car

Ancient Crimes in Ancient Times

This is the Colosseum in Rome. People called gladiators would fight in the Colosseum, and crowds of people would watch.

Ancient Rome was one of the biggest, busiest cities of its time. It was founded in 753 B.C. and it is thought that over a million people lived there at the height of its power. There were rich people, poor people, **SLAVES**, travellers – all sorts of people walked the streets. However, although there were many great things about Rome, there was also a lot of crime. When the Sun went down and night fell, the city became quite different...

From what was written down at the time, Rome seemed like a scary place. If a person wandered the dark streets, they might be beaten up and have their money stolen from them. People often emptied their chamber pots out of the window too – this meant that it could rain wee and poo at any moment. Rich people would only walk the streets at night if they had to, and even then they would take bodyguards. The rest of the time they would stay safe at home, surrounded by slaves and guard dogs.

According to some, Emperor Nero wore disguises and ran around at night, partying. It is said he would often get into fights and break into shops.

The Romans did not have a police force, but they did have groups of watchmen, called the vigiles. Their job was mainly to stop fires, but they would also look out for crimes being committed. Some of these vigiles were good people – there is a record of one watchman giving his life while rescuing people in a fire. However, some were bad. There is one story in A.D. 64 of vigiles **LOOTING** the city after a huge fire broke out.

Even with the vigiles, most people had to look out for themselves.

THE TWELVE TABLES

Roman laws were called the Twelve Tables. Here are some examples of the laws of the ancient Romans.

• If a witness tells lies in **COURT**, they will be thrown down from the Tarpeian Rock. The Tarpeian Rock was a steep cliff in the city of Rome.

• Nobody is allowed to hold meetings in the city after dark.

• It is against the law to kill a thief in the day, unless the thief attacks with a weapon. However, people were allowed to kill thieves at night.

• Dead people are not allowed to be buried or burned in the city.

Victor Lustig

Victor Lustig was one of the greatest conmen of all time. In his life, he had over 47 different names and backstories. He had dozens of different passports. He spent his life escaping from the police and pulling off some of the strangest crimes that you'll ever hear of. Lustig said that he was born in 1890, in the Austrian-Hungarian town of Hostinné. Once, he said he was the son of a wealthy mayor, while another time he said his parents were poor peasants. However, historians can find no record of Lustig ever being born at all.

Victor Lustig never held a gun; he used words as his weapon. He could trick people into giving him money by using his charm. He began as a pickpocket on the streets, and then became a burglar. Soon he was hustling – this meant tricking passers-by into betting money on a card game. However, Lustig was like a magician, and could change which cards appeared in the game to help him win.

Lustig had a big scar on his cheek, over six centimetres long (you can't charm everyone, it seems). He became known as 'The Scarred'.

THE EIFFEL TOWER

Lustig's most startling crime was carried out in 1925. In Paris, France, Lustig pretended to be a government worker, and invited some of the top **SCRAP METAL** companies to meet him at a hotel. He explained that the Eiffel Tower was going to be sold for scrap and whoever paid him the most money would get to have it. It worked – someone bought the Eiffel Tower from Lustig. Of course, when the man went to knock the Tower down, he was told that it was all nonsense. By this time Lustig was out of the country. A month later, Lustig came back and tried to sell the Eiffel Tower again!

MONEY MACHINES

Lustig then began selling money machines in the US. The machines would slowly print out $100 notes. People paid a lot of money for them. However, it turned out the notes were fake, and only a few were printed. But, as usual, Lustig was long gone. The US government became worried that the money machines would destroy the **ECONOMY**. Eventually, the US Secret Service was sent after Lustig. After a series of captures and escapes, the conman was sent to a high-security prison called Alcatraz.

Lustig's fake $100 notes were so realistic that he once tricked a sheriff in Texas with them. Nobody could tell the difference.

In 1935, Lustig was sent to the 'inescapable' Federal Detention Centre. However, Lustig cut through the bars and made a rope out of his bed sheets. He swung from the window and escaped.

The Salem Witch Trials

Not everyone convicted has actually committed a crime. From 1692 to 1693, a town called Salem in Massachusetts, in North America, carried out investigations to find out if some of the townspeople were witches. It all started when three girls aged between 9 and 11 began having **FITS**. They would scream, shake and roll around uncontrollably. When they were questioned by the **JUDGES**, they said that three witches had put a curse on them. They named three women of the town: Sarah Good, Sarah Osborne and Tituba. One of the women, Tituba, admitted it was true. She was probably hoping that she would be freed for agreeing with the judges, but all three women were thrown in jail.

The town panicked. Witches were people who were working with the devil, and the religious settlers of North America were scared. All over Massachusetts, people were being accused of witchcraft. Soon, a man called William Phipps set up a special court to deal with the witch problem.

This is the Witch House, in Salem. It was the home of the one of the judges.

The gallows was used for hangings.

The punishment for being a witch was hanging.

GALLOWS HILL

The first person to be hanged was a woman called Bridget Bishop. It took place somewhere that came to be called Gallows Hill. Soon, five more people were hanged, and then eight more the next month. One man, Giles Corey, was killed by being squashed between two heavy stones for two days until he died. In the court, people would babble and whimper. This was seen as a sign of a demonic spirit in the room. The people also said that they had dreamt about who was **GUILTY**. This was called spectral evidence, and it was used to prove that people were witches.

Eventually, a minister called Cotton Mather wrote a letter, begging everybody to stop panicking, and asking the court to stop listening to spectral evidence. The court agreed that this had all gone too far. Everybody in prison for witchcraft was let go. However, for many it was too late. The court admitted that those who were hanged were innocent and had never been witches in the first place.

Around 150 people were investigated to see if they were witches. 19 people were hanged.

The names of the innocent are written in stones in Salem today.

MARY PARKER
HANGED
SEPT. 22 1692

Medieval Torture

THE NAUGHTY CHAIR OF MEDIEVAL TIMES

There are all sorts of things that stop people committing crimes nowadays, such as police, security cameras and alarms. However, none of these existed far back in the past. Instead, people came up with the scariest, goriest and nastiest punishments they could think of to put the criminals off doing the crime. Here are just a few punishments from medieval times in Europe, between A.D. 476 and 1400.

TRIAL BY FIRE

To prove they were innocent, people might have been forced to pick up a red-hot iron bar. Their hands would then be bandaged up. After three days, the bandages were removed. If their burns were starting to heal, then they were innocent. If the burns looked the same, then they were guilty.

FLOGGING

If someone was accused of not working hard enough, they might be punished with flogging. This was where they were whipped, usually on the back, while their hands were tied up. This might have been done in front of people, or in a prison.

It turned out that no matter how nasty the punishments were, people still committed crimes.

CHOPPING STUFF OFF

A lot of the time, punishments involved chopping parts of the body off. For example, if a person was caught stealing, they might have their hands cut off. If someone was found guilty of murder, they might have their head cut off. Another punishment for murder was hanging – the criminal would have a rope tied around their neck, and would be dangled by that rope until they died. Sometimes they died of a broken neck, and sometimes they died because they couldn't breathe.

During these times, around three-quarters of all recorded crimes were theft.

THE STOCKS

If someone had cheated or been a nuisance to society, they would be put in the stocks, or the pillory. The criminal would be placed somewhere everybody could see them. Often, people threw rotten vegetables at those in the pillory or stocks. This punishment usually lasted a couple of days. However, sometimes worse things would be thrown at the trapped criminals, such as saucepans, stones, and dead cats and dogs. Sometimes the criminals could be killed this way.

The pillory held people's heads and wrists, while the stocks held their ankles.

29

Mystery Solved?

Were there any punishments that would explain our skeleton, here in the museum? If you said stealing during medieval times, well done! Thieves often had their hands cut off, which could explain why this skeleton is missing theirs. Also, the skeleton comes from around the medieval times – between 476 and 1400 A.D.

Perhaps this person lived in a medieval town. Maybe they lived a good life at first – they could have been a farmer growing vegetables. In their time off they may have wrestled with their friends and sung songs. However, one day something might have caught their eye, weapon. Thinking that nobody was looking, they stole it – but they were caught! Before they knew it, their hands were cut off! Well, at least they could still sing songs. If this was true, it would be one of many stories that survive through time and history and teach us about the past.

Glossary

CHEMIST a person who studies chemicals and carries out experiments

COMMANDED was in charge of (or to have given an order)

COMMIT carry out

CONFESSED admitted or owned up to

COURT a group of people brought together to settle criminal disputes

DISGUISES outfits that hide what someone really looks like, so they can't be recognised

ECONOMY the way trade and money is controlled and used by a country or region

EVIDENCE something that gives proof and can be used to give reason to believe in something

FEUD a strong, serious disagreement that lasts a very long time

FITS moments where someone shakes uncontrollably, often falling to the floor and being unconscious

GOVERNMENT a group of people with the authority to run a country and decide its laws

GUILTY responsible for a bad action or wrongdoing

HANGED dangled by a piece of rope tied around the neck until dead

INVESTIGATION an inquiry where facts are examined in order to find out the truth

JUDGES people chosen to make important decisions for cases in court

LOOTING to steal things, usually during a time of crisis

MOBS large crowds that are often violent

OUTLAW someone who lives a life that doesn't follow the law

PEASANTS poor land workers who belonged to the lowest social class

PRIMITIVE basic or early in development

PUNISHED when a person is hurt, forced to pay money, or sent away because of a crime they have committed

RECORDS documents or files which keep track of something

RELIGION the belief in and worship of a god or gods

SCRAP METAL old bits of metal that are broken down and used again

SENTENCED given a punishment by law

SLAVES people who have no freedom and are owned by other people

SMUGGLED to have illegally brought something in or out of a place

STOCKY someone whose physical characteristics are solid

TRAITS qualities or characteristics of a person

VIOLENT the use of force to physically hurt someone

WITNESSES people who were there at the time and swear to tell the truth about what happened

Index